Making a Difference

REDUCING

Rubbish

Sue Barraclough

W
FRANKLIN WATTS
LONDON•SYDNEY

This edition 2011

Franklin Watts
338 Euston Road
London NW1 3BH

Franklin Watts Australia
Level 17/207 Kent Street
Sydney NSW 2000

© 2006 Franklin Watts

Original concept devised by
Sue Barraclough and Jemima Lumley.

Editor: Adrian Cole
Designer: Jemima Lumley
Art director: Jonathan Hair
Special photography: Mark Simmons
Consultant: Helen Peake, Education Officer at
  The Recycling Consortium, Bristol

Acknowledgements:
The author and publisher wish to thank Helen Peake and the staff at
The Recycling Consortium. Images on pages 7tc, 8, 13t, supplied by
the national Recycle Now campaign (for more information on recycling
visit www.recyclenow.com). Chris Fairclough; page 9. Ava, Connie,
James, Romi, Ruby, Vincent and Tom for taking part.

A CIP catalogue record for this book is available
from the British Library.

ISBN: 978 1 4451 0607 6

Dewey Classification: 363.72'82

Printed in China

Franklin Watts is a division of Hachette Children's Books,
an Hachette UK company.
www.hachette.co.uk

Oldham
Council

Please return this book before the last date stamped.

You can renew this book in person at any library,
by calling Oldham Library on 0161 770 8000
or by visiting www.oldham.gov.uk/libraries

Contents

What is reducing?

Reducing means to make less. We need to reduce our rubbish.

Think before you throw things away, because many materials should not be in the bin.

The materials below in the green sections should not be put into a bin. They can be reused or recycled. We can also reduce rubbish by not creating so much of it.

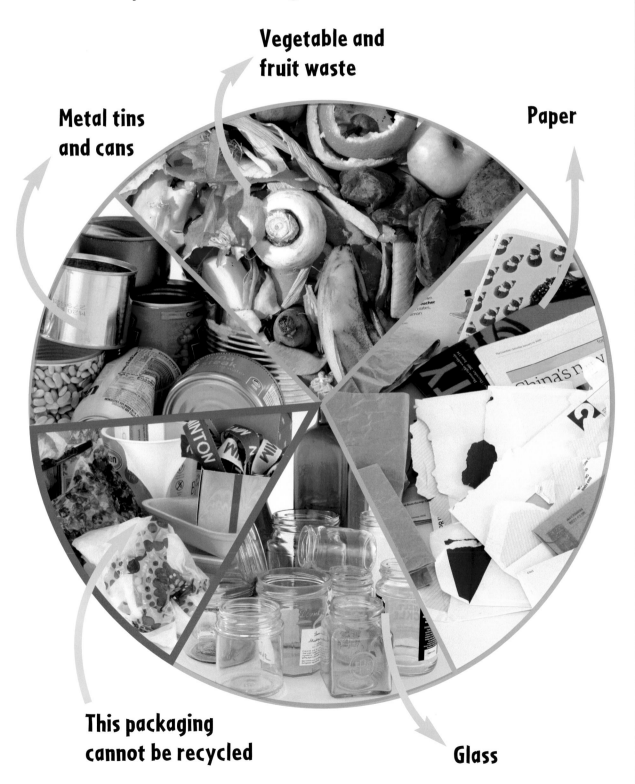

Vegetable and fruit waste

Metal tins and cans

Paper

This packaging cannot be recycled

Glass

Why reduce rubbish?

Most rubbish that you put into a bin is buried at a landfill site. We do not have enough room to carry on burying huge amounts of rubbish.

What you can do

Before you throw something away try to reuse it, or find someone else that can.

Rubbish like this can cause pollution to land, air and water. It can be dangerous for all living things.

Reducing packaging

Most of the things we buy are wrapped in packaging. Packaging is the box, the wrapping or the bag that you buy something in.

String

Boxes

Packets

Pots

Wrappers

Bags

Trays

Some packaging is useful because it stops food getting squashed or broken. Other packaging is there only to make something look good. Most packaging is usually thrown away.

When you buy something from a shop, think about the packaging. Is it made from recycled material? Can it be reused or recycled?

All this packaging is for a handful of beads! Some of the plastic could be reused and the cardboard can be recycled.

Take less rubbish home

At the shops you can help to choose things with less packaging. Your family will have less rubbish to recycle or throw away.

Help to choose loose vegetables and fruit. Lots of food has a plastic wrapper and tray that have to be thrown away.

What you can do

Some shops sell food without packaging. You can scoop out what you need. Avoid boxes and cartons if you can.

Think about rubbish

Think about rubbish when you go to the shops. Look out for things that have too much packaging.

Shopping tips to reduce rubbish:

Make a shopping list so you do not buy things you do not need.

Take bags with you to the shops – then you can say "no thank you" to plastic and paper bags.

Buy tins of pet food, not packets. The foil packets have to be thrown away. The tins can be recycled.

Buy big bottles of juice or squash. Using one big bottle, instead of two or three smaller ones, cuts down on rubbish.

Avoid plastic packaging. Choose items with packaging made of paper or glass. These can be recycled easily.

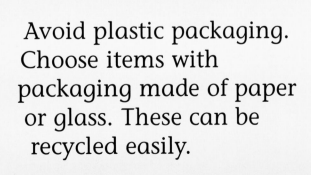

No rubbish lunchbox

If you have a packed lunch,
use a lunchbox with sections.
Then you do not have to wrap
anything up in packaging.

Drinks carton

Metal foil

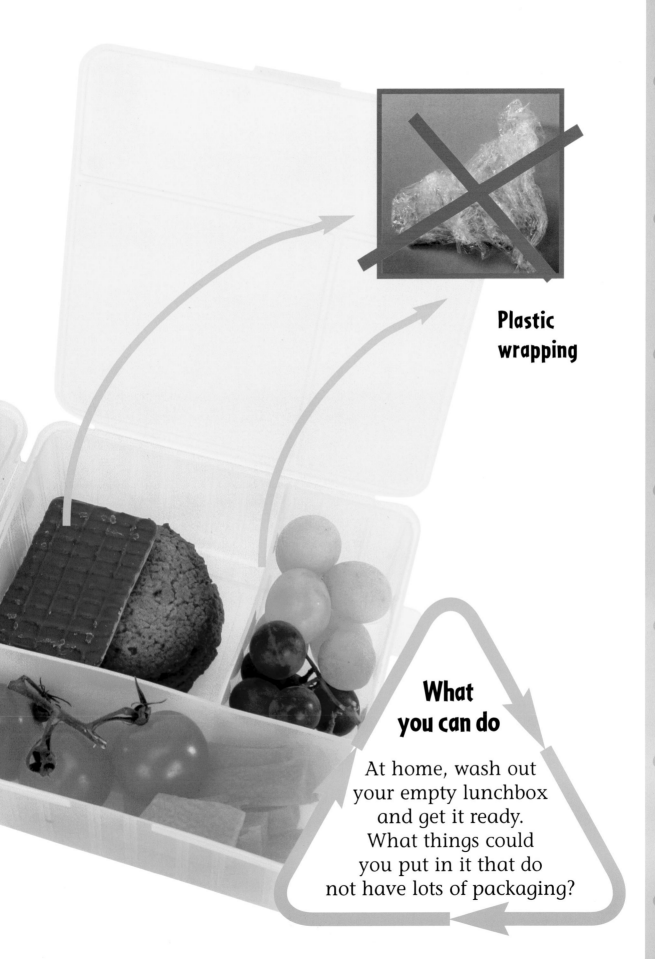

Plastic wrapping

What you can do

At home, wash out your empty lunchbox and get it ready. What things could you put in it that do not have lots of packaging?

Refills reduce rubbish

Think of all the bottles and cartons that get put in the bin every day.

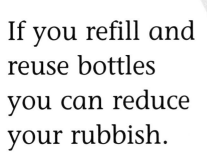

If you refill and reuse bottles you can reduce your rubbish.

18

Make a simple funnel using half an old plastic bottle. This makes refilling bottles much easier.

What you can do

Use a plastic bottle that can be refilled. If you take a bottle to school every day you will save five bottles or cartons in one week.

Make your own

If you make and bake your own food, you can cut down on some packaging.

Most food and takeaway packaging has to be thrown away.

Pizzas are easy and quick to make. See page 27 for a simple pizza recipe.

Making food is fun. Just think
about all the packaging you
won't have to throw away.

Grow your own food

Another good way to reduce rubbish is to grow your own food. You can use old packaging as seed trays.

Seeds

Look out for seeds in different fruits and vegetables.

You can buy packets of seeds to grow your favourite vegetables.

Cress

What you can do

Try growing cress seeds. Just sprinkle them on wet tissue.

Sorting out rubbish

When you have finished with something, do not just throw it into a rubbish bin. Sort and save glass, paper and metal for reusing or recycling.

A can crusher

Ask an adult to help you crush cans and tins. They will take up less room in your recycling box.

Put vegetable and fruit waste
into a compost bin or wormery.

Sort recycling into
storage boxes. It will
be easy to empty them
on collection day.

Glass

Metal

Paper

All sorts of packaging

Can you guess what was in this packaging? How could you reuse it?

1

2

3

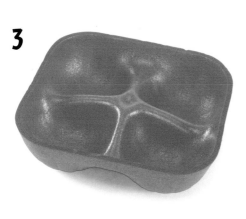

4

5
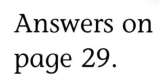

7

6

Answers on
page 29.

Make a pizza

It is easy to make your own pizza.
You can choose your own topping.
You won't have lots of packaging left over.

You will need:
• A pizza base mix.
(You could use some thick
slices of bread instead).
• Tomato puree.
• Cheese.
• Different toppings, such
as peppers and mushrooms.

1. Ask an adult to pre-heat the oven to 220°C /
gas mark 7.

2. Use a pizza base mix to make your pizza base.

3. Now spread over some tomato puree.

4. Next, cover with your toppings.
We chose peppers and slices of cheese.

5. Sprinkle some grated cheese on top.

6. Finally, ask an adult to bake your pizza
in the oven. Cook it for 20–25 minutes.

Find out more

Reducing rubbish is all about re-thinking rubbish. Some packaging protects our food and keeps it fresh, but a lot of packaging is not really needed. You can help to reduce rubbish by avoiding packaging that cannot be recycled or reused. Try not to buy products that have too much packaging.

www.wasteonline.org.uk
Click on the information button to find out waste facts and information on reducing rubbish at home.

www.resourcefutures.co.uk
Links to waste education resources.

www.ollierecycles.com.au/ club/puzz_sustain.htm
See if you can solve the planet watch word puzzle.

www.wwf.org.uk
Follow the 'how you can help' link to the 're-think your lifestyle' page. Look at the 'kids' link for quizzes and simple things you can do to make a difference.

www.factmonster.com
Type 'recycling' in the search box to find lots of useful links and recycling information.

www.recyclenow.com
Find out what you can recycle in your local area.

Glossary

Compost bin – a container used to store kitchen and garden waste where it breaks down.

Landfill site – a huge hole in the ground that is filled with rubbish.

Material – the substance something is made from. For example, paper is made from a material called wood.

Packaging – bottles, jars, cartons, boxes, bags, wrappings and containers. All these things can be made from materials such as paper, glass and plastic.

Pollution – making something dirty or poisoning it.

Recycle – using something again or make it into something new.

Recycling collection scheme – a system where materials to be recycled are collected from the kerbside.

Seeds – the parts of a plant that can grow into new plants.

Wormery – a special container to hold worms and waste. The waste is eaten by the worms.

Answers to the quiz on page 26: 1 – eggs, use to store coins, etc; 2 – a CD, use to keep computer discs in; 3 – fruit, use as a paint mixing palette; 4 – strawberry jam, use as a pencil pot; 5 – fish, recycle; 6 – cakes, fill with water and seed to feed birds outside; 7 – apple juice, some cartons cannot be recycled or reused.

Index

About this book

Making A Difference: Reducing Rubbish encourages children to think about the problems of throwing away lots of rubbish, especially packaging.

The book introduces a range of first-hand experiences that children can use to extend their knowledge and understanding of the world. The opening pages focus on the idea that many of the things we throw in the bin can be recycled.

Pages 8 and **9** explore why it is important to reduce our rubbish. Discuss the idea that all the rubbish we throw away will be burned or buried.
Use **pages 10** and **11** to think about packaging, and then use pages **12–15** to think about different ideas to reduce rubbish while you shop.
Pages 16–17 explore the ideal of having no rubbish at all to throw-away, with a no-rubbish lunchbox.

Pages 18–23 look at some practical ideas and projects for reducing rubbish.
Pages 24–28 take a look at simple ways to sort out rubbish, and how children can get involved.

These simple ideas can form the foundations of thinking about our impact on the planet, saving natural resources and whether we are living sustainably.